IMAGES FROM
A LIMESTONE LANDSCAPE

A Journey into the
Punakaiki-Paparoa Region

By Craig Potton and Andy Dennis

IMAGES FROM
A LIMESTONE LANDSCAPE

A Journey into the Punakaiki-Paparoa Region

By Craig Potton and Andy Dennis

CRAIG POTTON PUBLISHING

DEDICATION

This book is dedicated to all those people, both on the West Coast and from other parts of New Zealand, who over the past decade or so have contributed to the campaign to ensure that the land which has now become the Paparoa National Park is to be preserved in perpetuity as Nature designed it.

Special thanks to Bruce and Carol Knight of Punakaiki.

PUBLISHED BY: Craig Potton Publishing,
PO Box 555, Nelson, New Zealand.

DESIGN: Donna Hoyle.

COLOUR SEPARATIONS: Robert MacLeod,
Lithograph Laboratory, Wellington, New Zealand.

PRINT SUPERVISION: Mostyn Hainsworth.

PRINTING: Printgroup, Wellington Ltd,
New Zealand.

First published in 1987 (hardback). ISBN 0:908802-00-5.
This edition (softback) published in 1997. ISBN 0-908802 38-2.

CONTENTS

AT TRUMANS BEACH

For Daniel

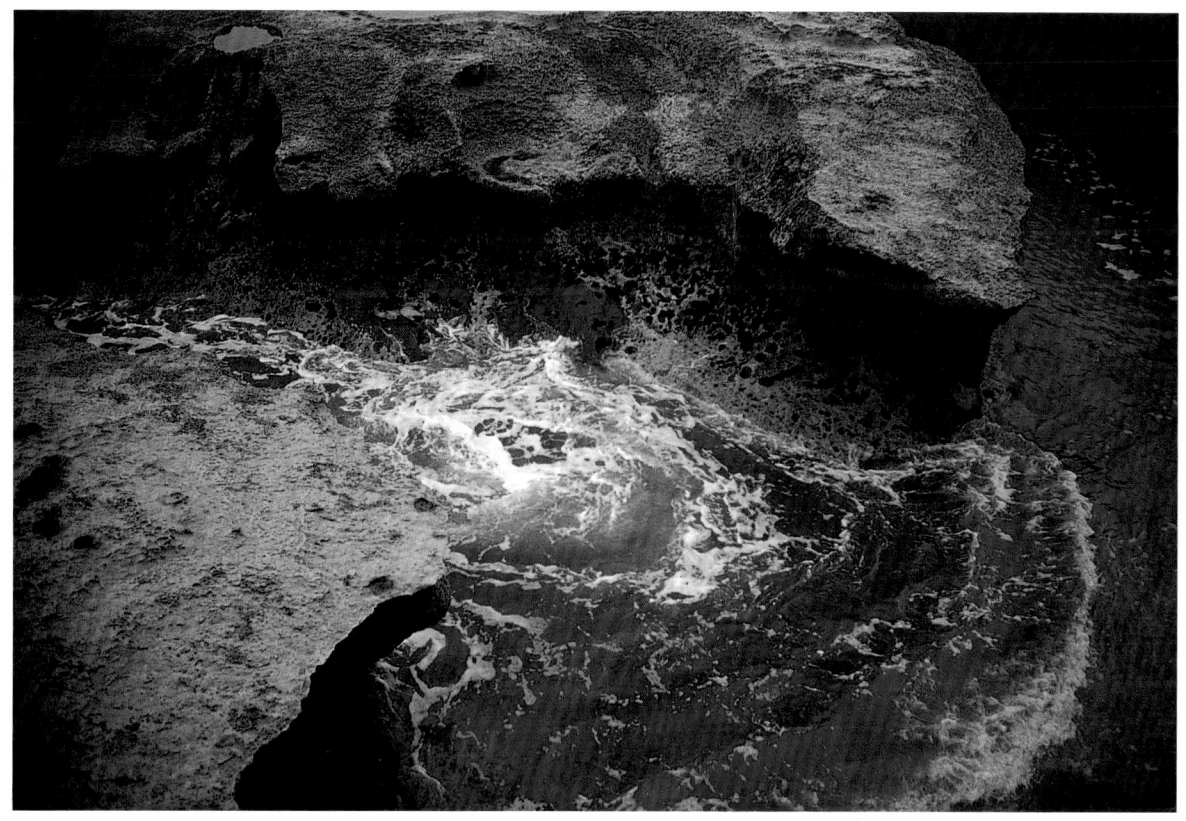

High tide. The seething thunder
of the waves' white fury
recoils upon itself. A smoke
of spume cascades
from wet black rock.
Waves grind abrasive sands
at roots of cliffs
where flax and moss let fall
drops of sweet water to the salt
harsh shaping of new worlds.

Calmly you distill a new creation,
with coloured brush command a fury,
outmaster waves, resolve
the flux of time, the lifted mind
a centre of chosen power.

Only the artist rides this chaos
reining its potency, finding his peace
deriving order from tumult,
breaking the rock
to free the imprisoned dream.

PETER HOOPER

Streamside reflections, Fox River.

INTRODUCTION

TOWARDS the end of 1980 I rented a little cottage at Carters Beach near Westport on the West Coast of the South Island, and began to contemplate, explore and fossick out information on the Paparoa Range, the chain of coastal mountains between the Grey and Buller rivers, which was then beginning to capture attention as a potential region for a new national park. The idea of a "Paparoa National Park" was first developed and promoted by the conservation movement mainly out of concern for the fate of the lowland forests surrounding the range, which by 1980 were being comprehensively earmarked for production and invaded ever more deeply by logging roads.

In spite of the publicity and controversy that this park proposal was attracting, I soon discovered that much of the region was more or less *terra incognita* to the wider public, including most of the people living on its fringes. Although plenty of hot air about "locking up assets" was wafting out of the local hotels, council chambers and editorial offices at the time, the only people who seemed to have any real depth of firsthand knowledge of this particular "asset" were a few widely scattered scientists, an occasional forest service ranger, and a handful of local hunters, possumers and cavers. Mostly, therefore, I had no real alternative but to find things out for myself.

As I slowly began to unravel some of the secrets of its rivers and ridges, its densely forested valleys and craggy uplands, I found myself spending more and more time in the beautiful but often bewildering limestone region which extends as a broad, shallow trough (or syncline) for about 30 km along the western flank of the range. For several years I had been travelling the coastal fringe of this limestone country fairly frequently, invariably enchanted by its succession of little bays, rocky headlands and thick tangles of lush green vegetation, but only mildly curious about its striking natural architecture, with the notable exception of the strange formations of "Pancake Rocks" at Punakaiki. I suppose that like most people I was usually in too much of a hurry, and when I did travel less urgently found ample enough distraction in the marvellous coastal scenery and shifting moods of the sea. At all events, I gave little serious thought to what else might lie hidden beneath the rim of the sea cliffs, buried deep in the forests, or concealed behind the high band of limestone bluffs which effectively isolate the narrow strip of coastal land. But when I did finally begin to examine this hidden country more closely, it quickly became apparent that the weird symmetry of Punakaiki's Pancake Rocks was not so much a rare accident of Nature's artistry, as a

Pancake Rocks, Punakaiki.

token of a kind of landscape eccentricity which occurs again and again throughout the whole of this western Paparoa limestone region, not only above the ground but beneath it as well.

A year or so later the results of my wider wanderings, discoveries and ruminations emerged as THE PAPAROAS GUIDE, which I published in cooperation with the Native Forests Action Council. When the book began to attract favourable comment, and, somewhat more importantly, helped to entice people to undertake more thoughtful and lingering visits to this part of the West Coast, I felt a considerable sense of achievement. And yet I remained vaguely dissatisfied about the way the book had finally evolved. Towards the end of the introduction - which, as usual, was written last - I tried to express these feelings by writing that perhaps my greatest regret in assembling a guidebook of this kind had been that in choice of emphasis "aesthetics have regularly had to yield to the more mundane business of conveying information. There were times when a few illustrations mixed with a delicate measure of philosophy, lyrical poetry and pioneer epigram seemed more suited to do justice to the many moods of the Paparoas than the extensive descriptions contained in this book. Indeed, at times the very idea of attempting to reduce landscapes and life-systems to words felt like a clumsy intrusion on a wild and mysterious world."

Behind these thoughts lay not only the frustrations of trying to find words for sights and sentiments which had often seemed to be indescribable, but also the fact that the need to be always scribbling and recording had managed at times to distance me from the simple pleasures of wandering through wild places uncluttered and free. I was also becoming increasingly aware that the emerging book was getting weightier and weightier in terms of text, but remaining rather light in accompanying illustrations, and that with one or two notable exceptions (like Marion van Dijk's black and white studies of the Pancake Rocks) the photographs I had managed to assemble had not really begun to do justice to the shapes and moods of a landscape which obviously held such a wealth of aesthetic possibilities for patient and sensitive photography.

The shoestring budget on which THE PAPAROAS GUIDE was produced was undoubtedly the main reason why a greater range of colour photographs could not have been included. But the truth is also that up to that time the aims and efforts of myself and my usual tramping companions in the art of photography were still fairly limited. To be sure, most of us usually carried a camera along on our trips and maybe an extra lens or two, but rarely were such advanced items of equipment as tripods, polarising filters or umbrellas seen in the canyons and creekbeds. Moreover, well aware of the whims of the West Coast climate, we generally did our best to time our more ambitious explorations to coincide with periods of settled sunny weather, optimum conditions for following the rivers, getting lost in the forests, or clambering along the

Detail of shore platform near Perpendicular Point.

10

The native odd-leaved orchid
Aporostylis bifolia.

Part of the small life of the forest.

tops, but much less likely to provide the subtleties of atmosphere and light on which artistic photography is often so dependent. When I look back on that first busy summer in the Paparoas I realise too that it was not just the fact that we had less skill as photographers in those early days, but that we were simply so hell-bent on covering the country and exploring every hidden nook and cranny that the patience, perseverance and probably the solitude required to begin to capture the "many moods of the Paparoas" on film were not then the highest of our priorities.

The bundle of vagrant scribblings which emerged from this summer and autumn sojourn on the West Coast finally became a book at Craig Potton's house in Nelson during the following winter. At that time Craig was working for the Native Forests Action Council, and among other duties had landed the task of keeping me chained to the typewriter until the project was finished. About this time too he had begun to dabble more seriously in photography as an art form rather than as a means of merely recording plants, animals, people and places. Accordingly, as he and I sifted and resifted through the collections of drawings and photographs which we had managed to beg, borrow or otherwise acquire in our quest for illustrations, it became apparent to us that adequate though some of this material was for guidebook purposes, it had barely begun to scratch the surface of a more aesthetic approach. Somewhere along the line we realised that the production of this particular guidebook was not so much an end as a beginning, and when the chaos of publishing deadlines was behind us we resolved to return as often as we could to the Punakaiki coastline, the Paparoa mountains and the hidden country in between. But from now on instead of always trying to discover what lay beyond the next bend in the river or bump on the ridge we would travel more patiently in search of shapes in the rock, patterns in the forest, or accidents of light on the sea cliffs and canyon walls.

Many times since then we have found ourselves back in this part of the West Coast, clambering along the coastal platforms, exploring deeper into the creeks and caves and canyons, turning aside at random from the tracks and creekbeds into the dense forests and climbing now and then onto the misty tops. Often we have deliberately planned these trips to coincide with periods of unsettled weather, but all the same I cannot recall a single instance when we have come away disappointed. If it did sometimes happen that we were driven off the tops by storms, or the rivers were too high, or the light in the forest not quite right, then that simply gave us the excuse, if we ever really needed one, to plan a swift return. Yet somehow, regardless of the weather or the season, we always seemed to get good photographs. Perhaps this is because when other parts of the region get cut off by the weather, places of easy access along the coast experience some of their best displays of light and anger. Or perhaps it is simply because this whole remarkable landscape retains so much of its magic and mystery throughout all of its many moods.

IMAGES FROM A LIMESTONE LANDSCAPE is a selection of the photographic spoils of these expeditions, not only through the western Paparoas karst region, but also (in blatant defiance of the title of the book, but for reasons which will be explained later) onto the adjacent granitic mountains of the Paparoa Range itself. We have also included a few short essays to help explain some of our own sentiments and the general background from which these images have been drawn; but there is no intention in this book to provide any kind of comprehensive description of the region, either visual or verbal, and it is certainly not meant to serve as a guidebook or handbook. Indeed, if it has any real message to convey, it is probably the simple but easily forgotten truth that things and places of great beauty are often kept hidden from us as much by the limitations which we carry within ourselves as by the obstacles which Nature may happen to have placed in our path. Endless variations on the main thematic threads which run through these pages are out there for anyone to find, sometimes within a couple of minutes of the road, sometimes only after a day's hard struggle through untracked forest. All that is really needed (besides of course a map, compass, guidebook, lunch, spare jersey, parka, insect repellent, camera, tripod, polarising filter, umbrella, etc. etc.) is a willingness to abandon your carefully planned schedule, to get away from the car (and the further the better), to go happily exploring in drizzle as well as in sunshine, and to get lost in the positive sense of getting lost, by surrendering yourself to the sounds of the sea, the music of the tumbling streams, the smell of the forest and the intuitive poetic impulses which are hibernating away in each and every soul.

Notwithstanding the preceding homily, some people may still be irked by the fact that we do not always identify, or specify closely, the locations at which these photographs have been taken. The simple answer to that is to point out that certain fragile parts of the landscape need the protection of anonymity (caves are an obvious example), and it is not our intention to provide new tourist traps in hitherto secret places. Indeed, to be honest, such moments of passing melancholy which have arisen in the course of our wanderings have often derived from the realisation that some of the precious wilderness quality of places like this Paparoas limestone country is bound to be surrendered by each new wave of publicity given to the area, regardless of how carefully or sensitively this is done. At times, therefore, we have been thankful that we were following the course of nameless streams, or that ours were the only footmarks high on the ridge or on the forest floor.

But there are other good reasons for restraining the commentary in a book like this. In seeking to convey an aesthetic view of the natural world, some photographs ought to be left to speak for themselves, to ask their own questions and suggest their

Fruits of a kiekie vine.

12

Gentian and sundew near an alpine tarn.

own answers. We do not always want an Attenborough peering over our shoulder or a Bellamy sitting on every stone, helpful though their cheerful anecdotes and explanations very often are. It is surely just as important that sometimes we search things out for ourselves, not only in actual first-hand contact with the landscape, but also in reflections of it supplied by poets, photographers and artists.

And so to more mundane matters. A few words should be added in these introductory remarks about the nature of our individual contributions to the common project. At the end of the day the majority of the photographs have come from Craig's cameras and most of the words struggled out of my battered little typewriter. But in a wider sense the venture remains very much a joint one. Virtually all the photographs have come from trips which we have undertaken together and we generally had little trouble in agreeing where we should go and what we should look for.

Craig's greatly increased use of large format cameras over the past couple of years has meant that I have regularly lugged a share of his heavy gear up misty ridges and through muddy cave passages. If a brolly had to be held in the rain, I usually held it. Or if plungers got lost (and they did – two in the space of about half an hour once at the "Hole In The Wall") or tripods maimed (and they did – limestone covered with algae is a lethal surface) I usually let Craig have first choice on whatever gear had managed to survive unscathed. "What a wholly decent companion" I hear you say; but it wasn't simply altruism that prompted these noble gestures. Besides being the owner of a rather more modest selection of photographic equipment than Craig, I was also usually much more parsimonious with film, and generally less patient (but I hope decreasingly so) in the pursuit of artistic results.

For the first ten or a dozen trips all our photography was done with 35mm cameras, Craig using several Nikons and I a trusty old Pentax Spotmatic. Gradually, however, Craig switched more and more to working with larger format cameras (mostly a Pentax 6x7) and although we had been very pleased with a lot of the early results on 35mm film, most of the more tempting subjects were eventually re-photographed in larger format. The large format professional film used seems to create less contrast and be more tolerant of light variation. It is also considerably better at handling the unusual greens of New Zealand native forests. There is obviously also exciting scope for the use of a view camera in this kind of country, but that particular photographic adventure will have to wait until we have worked out how to use such a complex device. All 35mm photographs were taken with Kodachrome 64, and large format with professional Ektachrome 64.

In the final analysis the success of our photographic journeys probably resulted from a mixture of my restless mobility, which undoubtedly helped us to discover many new locations and subjects, and Craig's contemplative patience, which usually ensured that they got recorded on film as he wanted them, if not on one trip then on another, or another, or another. It speaks volumes for the kind of country it is that we could return again and again to any of our favourite haunts and almost always find something new and exciting, often startlingly so. From my own point of view I am sure that the adventurous aspect of the journeys always remained important, but in the course of discovering and recording these images (and many, many others) I also slowly learned to look at them (and for them) in a different kind of way.

A decade before I wrote THE PAPAROAS GUIDE I was given, while living for a year in the United States, a little volume of wilderness photography, poetry and philosophy called ON THE LOOSE, written by Terry and Renny Russell and published by the Sierra Club. A good deal of it was just thoughtful adventuring, but one or two of the photographs were really superb. So too were some of the accompanying sentiments. Alongside a close-up of wave-patterned mudstone cut almost like deliberate paving slabs the caption read: "So you went to the Louvre; what did you see?" And accompanying a study of purple rocks and red desert sands was a bow to all that is beautiful in natural landscape in the humble acknowledgement: "After the first artist only the copyist".

Perhaps reflections like these help a little to explain our aims and intentions in this book. They do not seem to me to be thoughts which belittle the value of museums and art galleries, or depreciate the creative contribution of those who find their inspiration in the wilds. Rather they are sentiments which invite us to go with our eyes and minds open to places like this limestone landscape, where wind stirs in the forests and mist weaves patterns in the canyons and water goes scurrying on strange journeys. Just gentle reminders too that in all wild places' photography even the most inspired results are truly only images – reflections of the work of water on rock, the subtleties of light, and the ingenuity of all living things.

Streamside reflections, Fox River.

OPPOSITE: Natural bridges, Waggon Creek.

THE EVOLUTION OF KARST LANDSCAPES

IN an epoch known to geologists as the Oligocene, which lasted from 38 until 26 million years ago, proto New Zealand would have been quite unrecognizable as the ancestor of the land we inhabit today. Mountains were entirely absent from what was merely a low-lying archipelago of islands, the coastline of which bore no resemblance whatsoever to the present geographical layout, with seas covering many places which have since been raised up as new land areas and vice versa. The evidence indicates also that throughout much of this period the climate was unusually warm and benign, and as a result marine life abounded in peaceful coastal waters. This combination of mild climate and low-lying terrain also ensured that processes of erosion were reduced to a fairly languid pace. If geomorphologists had existed in those times they would undoubtedly have found things for the most part dreadfully dull. All the same, beneath the placid, conservative exterior of the Oligocene the seeds of future landscape eccentricity were secretly being sown.

In shallow coastal waters which were nevertheless far enough out from land to be largely free of sand and pebbles, thick strata of sediments made up mainly from organic matter were slowly accumulating and compacting. The principal ingredients in these sediments were not sand and mud but shells and skeletons of marine organisms, both of which are rich in calcium carbonate or what is loosely known as lime. Subsequent burial under great thicknesses of younger sediments for 30 million years slowly hardened these Oligocene beds into limestone, until eventually stirrings of the Earth's crust associated with the uplift of our present mountain ranges raised them up from their ancestral seas.

Initially these limestone beds would have covered vast areas of the new land emerging from the sea, including the whole of the Paparoa Range and probably the whole northern half of the South Island. But as the pulse of uplift increased during the last two or three million years so too did the efficiency of the eroding forces, with the result that most of the limestones and other Tertiary sediments were eventually stripped away from the much more ancient basement rocks and recycled back to the sea. Yet here and there, in widely scattered locations, pockets of limestone did manage to survive, and along with them some of the most beautiful and bizarre of all our diverse landforms.

In these endless cycles of sedimentation, uplift and erosion which manufacture new rocks, shape our present landscapes, and ensure that not even mountains can last

One of several large fluted overhangs near the bottom of Truman Track.

OPPOSITE: The Hole in the Wall, a huge natural arch cut by an unnamed tributary of the Nile River.

for ever, limestones have come up with a special trick of their own. Besides being subject to the normal destructive processes of weathering and mechanical erosion, limestones also actually dissolve in water. This means that the forces which slowly attack, shape and remove limestone have more scope to work than in the case of other types of rock, and that erosion can proceed in situations which would be impossible in the case of insoluble rocks. Striking examples of these special qualities are seen in the way honeycombs of caves develop in many limestone regions, often containing some of the strangest and most stunningly beautiful of all natural creations in rock.

Dissolution of rocks with a high content of calcium carbonate occurs when these rocks come into contact with rainwater made slightly acidic by picking up carbon dioxide from the atmosphere, or, far more effectively, from biological sources like leaf litter and humus on the forest floor. As this water gradually etches its way down through the joints and fractures in the calcite rock, distinctive landforms slowly evolve which reflect both the soluble nature of the rock and the emerging subterranean patterns of drainage: underground channels take over from surface streams; valleys are left blind and abandoned; basins become self-draining; sinkholes and slots pock-mark the landscape; deep gorges and canyons develop with curiously fashioned cliffs, columns, arches, overhangs and alcoves; and all manner of weird carvings, runnels and flutings are found on the exposed surfaces of the rock. Beneath the ground complex networks of subterranean shafts, passages and caverns gradually develop, decorated here and there by patient works of art which in these galleries of slow change are formed by what is the exception rather than the rule – a depositional process involving limestone and water rather than a destructive one. And finally, in places where these soluble rocks are in contact with the sea, wind and waves have their own robust notions about just what kinds of architectural eccentricities are appropriate for limestone sections of the coastline.

Landscapes of soluble rocks containing underground drainage and other features like those just listed are often referred to as "karst", the name of a limestone district in Yugoslavia where much of this kind of distinctive scenery is found. Karst regions in New Zealand occur either in these mid-Tertiary limestones, or in very much older calcareous Paleozoic rocks, the most notable of which is the belt of Ordovician marble about 500 million years old, which stretches southwards from the Takaka Hill over Mt Arthur and Mt Owen, and contains the longest and deepest cave systems in the country. (Marbles are simply more ancient limestones which have compacted and recrystalized as a result of aeons of great pressure and heat, deep in the Earth's crust; but the chemical composition of the rock remains the same.) Some similar features are also found on glaciers (hence the term "glacier karst") where meltwaters percolating through the glaciers dissolve the ice to form moulins, sinkholes, vanishing streams and

Eroded limestone in the Fox River narrows near Dilemma Creek.

Sea-eroded limestone, Pancake Rocks.

Sculpted cliff face formed by progressive stream down-cutting.

ice caves in more or less the same way as happens in limestone landscapes, only very much more rapidly.

Optimum conditions for karstification occur where the limestone is massive, rich in calcium carbonate, and full of joints and fractures, and where the relief is bold, the rainfall high, and the vegetation prolific. Generally the western Paparoas limestone belt meets all these conditions more than adequately. Many of the most striking local landforms are found in a highly calcareous band of Potikohua (the Maori name for the Fox River) Limestone with an average calcium carbonate content of about 90%. The dense vegetation covering this fertile limestone country allows the percolating waters to pick up plenty of carbon dioxide, while the generous rainfall (about 2000 mm a year at Punakaiki) and bold relief ensure that these dissolving waters move frequently and rapidly through the system.

Striking though the resulting scenery is, much of the result of karstification in this part of the country remains deeply and anonymously buried beneath a covering of soils and gravels and a dense mantle of rain forest which blankets the land from the brink of the coastal cliffs to high on the Paparoa Range. Of necessity, therefore, most of our images have been drawn from those places where the underlying shape of the land breaks through this concealing covering – the margins of the sea, the beds and banks of rivers and streams, the vertical cliffs and canyon walls, and of course the caves. Many of these places are regularly subject to quite dramatic changes, not in the limestone landforms themselves, but in how much of them is exposed or concealed at any one time, as stormy seas, flooded rivers and landslips shift large amounts of gravel, sand, mud and forest debris in and out of all manner of nooks and crannies in the bedrock.

In our own life spans these changes will constantly alter the details but not the basic character of this limestone landscape. But if we shut our eyes and slip into a geological time-scale it is not hard to envisage former caves where there are now canyons, ancient carved shorelines (perhaps even past Pancake Rocks) still lying buried in the forests behind old uplifted beaches, and indeed all manner of past, present and future eccentricites secretly stored away throughout the whole of this limestone region, each awaiting some chance combination of climatic, erosive or tectonic events to expose them on the surface.

A sequence of reflections of clean limestone revealed along the banks of the Fox River during a period of minimal flow.

Mudstone shapes in the tidal chasm at the mouth of Bullock Creek.

Eroded limestone in the Fox River narrows near Dilemma Creek.

JOURNEYS AND IMAGININGS BY THE SEA.

AT the beginning of May 1846, in the course of exploring the northern section of the West Coast for the Nelson Provincial Government, Charles Heaphy and Thomas Brunner crossed the granite headland of Cape Foulwind and gazed southwards along the Paparoa coastline. In spite of the dangers and privations that they had already experienced and the obvious difficulties which still lay ahead, they were enraptured by the scene before them. With the "picturesque boat harbour of Tauranga" in the foreground, and the highest peaks of the Southern Alps rising above the distant sea horizon "like ice islands lying off the coast", Heaphy was moved to describe the whole prospect as "one of the prettiest views in the world".

Fourteen years later, with the West Coast still more or less undiscovered country (at least as far as Europeans were concerned), pioneer geologist Julius von Haast set off northwards from the mouth of the Grey River to re-examine this same stretch of coastline. Once again he was blessed with a gloriously fine day at the start of winter. Again, like Heaphy and Brunner heading in the opposite direction, Haast and his companions had to cross a major headland (Point Elizabeth) to gain an unimpeded view of the coast ahead. And again, when they finally beheld the Paparoa coastline stretching away to "the low hills of the Miko" on the horizon, they too were enraptured. As they descended to the beach near Rapahoe, Haast revelled in the spectacle of the restless waves of the deep blue sea beating against the "perpendicular cliffs at the foot of the Paparoa mountain chain" as well as the "numerous picturesque islands" close to them. Like Heaphy and Brunner (and no doubt countless thousands of subsequent travellers) Haast felt this was one of the most beautiful of all coastlines, and likened it to the stretch of the Riviera "between Genoa and Nizza (Nice), celebrated for its beauty, and to which alone it can be compared".

For a number of reasons these two diary entries had seemed like a logical starting point for my own reflective journeys into the landscape we have chosen for this book. Enabling me, as it were, to set off along the beaches in the esteemed company of these earliest European explorers, whose accounts of the shape of the coastline and the general character of this part of the West Coast have played a significant part in my own explorations and imaginings, and with whom I should accordingly very much like to discuss a number of matters when swollen rivers, perpendicular cliffs and dense tangles of coastal vegetation give us some respite. (I would like to be able to say the same about the Maori travellers who preceded them, but unfortunately their errands

Driftwood, Pororari Beach.

OPPOSITE: Pancake Rocks, Punakaiki.

and adventures have not been recorded.) What initially fascinated me in the accounts of Heaphy, Brunner and Haast were the glimpses they gave me of what this coast was like in its wilderness condition, and of how men so far from home had managed to cope with the exigencies of pioneer exploration. But as I pondered the contents of their journals more deeply other themes important to our present aims began to emerge from their accounts, perhaps not unlike the way this landscape itself has a habit of revealing a much more complex and intriguing character with close and patient examination.

To begin with, I began to notice how positive aesthetic response to aspects of the landscape tended to be expressed in terms of the scenery being "pretty" or "romantic" or "picturesque", not only for general panoramas like those from Cape Foulwind or Point Elizabeth, but also for certain individual landforms. Thus, in the course of his journey along the central section of the coastline bordering the main karst region, Haast described the Razorback as "a most picturesque headland, partly undermined by the action of waves". And following a typically ecstatic description of Dolomite Point from the beach to the north (limestone rocks containing "very nice caves"; their summits "crowned with superb vegetation, amongst which the nikau palm stretched its graceful crown"; the sea "dashing against the foot of the cliffs" etc.) he summed up the scene by writing that "the whole landscape had a most romantic aspect".

To some extent the recurrence of this kind of response was a product of the fact that Heaphy, Brunner and Haast had all grown up in Europe during the full flowering of the Romantic Era, although even today such descriptions would still be more than acceptable for many aspects of the Paparoa coastline, especially in fine weather. It is however one of the major themes of this book that much that is beautiful in this landscape transcends the merely pretty, romantic or picturesque. And further, that there are many aesthetic rewards to be experienced in conditions which are very much the antithesis of those which smiled so benignly on Heaphy, Brunner and Haast, when they first set eyes on the Paparoa coastline and gazed in rapture at what they saw.

As I became increasingly familiar with their day-to-day routine of advancing through un-mapped terrain, finding and preserving food, and improvising shelter, a second line of metaphysical musing began to intrude into my thoughts on these more mundane matters. I found myself regularly reflecting upon the thought that when travelling through this part of the West Coast, all these explorers faced at least a month's hard walking over exceedingly difficult country to return to the nearest European settlements. Moreover, even by the time of Haast's journey in 1860, there was still virtually no sea traffic in this part of the country and no Maori settlements north of the Mawhera Pa at the mouth of the Grey River. The more I speculated on this question of "distance from home", the more I was reminded of the fact that the

Bull kelp on a shore platform.

Cliff-edge patch of jointed rushes, Truman Track.

New roots in coastal flax.

caves and caverns, fluted cliffs and intricate shore platforms below Truman Track are today no more than a quarter of an hour's easy walking from the coastal highway. And the most famous landforms in the whole of this region, the Blowholes and Pancake Rocks on Punakaiki's Dolomite Point, are in reality a mere five minutes from the comfort of the car or bus, a nice cup of tea and the latest cricket scores.

How does this matter of distance, both in space and in thought, from things like comfort, security and home (usually summed up in the term "civilisation", though some might disagree!) affect the way we relate to landscape? In a book called ARCTIC DREAMS (of which a little more anon) northern wanderer Barry Lopez concluded that: "The reluctant traveller, brooding about events at home, is oblivious to the landscape. And no one is quite as alert as an indigenous hunter who is hungry." I know myself that on a tramp along the crest of the Paparoa Range, insulated from the concerns of civilisation by a day's journey on foot (usually across untracked country) I am undeniably more "alert to" (or perhaps "in tune with") certain aspects of the landscape than I am, for example, on a regular evening stroll along Pororari Beach. And while Heaphy, Brunner and Haast were not exactly "indigenous hunters" (although Kehu and other of their Maori companions were), they were a long way from events at home, forced to live almost entirely off the land, and frequently very, very hungry. Were they thus, I wonder, more alert to the landscape than we are today? And if so, then in what respects?

At the end of my introduction to THE PAPAROAS GUIDE I paid tribute to "Charles Heaphy, Thomas Brunner, Julius Haast and other explorers who came early to these parts with their eyes and tattered notebooks always open. . ." And while I still have no doubts whatsoever that these men were constantly alert to the landscape, day and night, week after difficult week, closer scrutiny of what they chose to record raises some interesting questions.

I could not help noticing, for example, that Heaphy in fact devotes very little space to the central limestone section of the Paparoa coastline, whose range of striking landforms (and picturesque settings) has since made it a focus of tourist attention, and from which most of the coastal images in our book have been drawn. (By "central limestone section" I mean the stretch of coast from north of the Miko Cliffs – or Perpendicular Point – to south of the Razorback. In fact, only at Dolomite Point is the rock actually in contact with the sea classified by geologists as limestone. But the rest is mostly a highly calcareous sandstone or mudstone, both of which behave in many of the same eccentric ways as the purer limestone strata.) I thought it strange that although Heaphy's account includes the famous description of their terrifying ascent of the Miko Cliffs on rotting ladders of ropey rata and flax, the total space given over to this leg of their journey was less than 400 words. (Ah yes, I hear you say, but writing up a diary in those conditions can't have been particularly easy. To which I would respond by pointing out that a few days earlier Heaphy had written half as much again on the esoteric indulgence of bush epicurism, especially the joys of dining on roast weka!) What makes all this even more intriguing is the fact that although Heaphy is probably better remembered today as a landscape painter rather than as an explorer, this brief page in his journal contains no aesthetic comment on the scenery whatsoever. (The "limestone landscape" page that is; the "roast weka" passage is one long eulogy!)

Even the ebullient and frequently verbose Haast appears to have been so preoccupied with his party's problems in ascending and descending the difficult headlands along this stage of their journey that he too failed to mention some of the most striking features of the local landscape. To some extent I can understand all these explorers missing both the Pancake Rocks and the strange architecture below Truman Track – they simply had so much trouble with the "interwoven tissue of kiekie and supplejacks" back from the brink of both of these headlands, that there can have been little incentive to detour seawards through more of the same merely to check out the view! But it is rather more difficult to account for a geologist and explorer as "alert to the landscape" as Haast undoubtedly was failing to mention features like the huge parallel flutings on Perpendicular Point, or the graphic entrances to the canyons of the Pororari River and Bullock Creek which so dominate the landward view from the sandspit of Pororari Beach, along which his path very obviously lay. Especially since the major focus of his voluminous and often quite detailed report was: "A Topographical and Geological Exploration of the Western Districts of Nelson Province".

The only conclusion that I can offer is that certain levels of aesthetic response may be more likely when one is relieved, to some extent, of the anxieties of staying warm, dry, safe and well fed, or go unreported unless one has the leisure (and also the equipment) to record them. I am reminded that a significant proportion of the photographs in this book – not only of the coast, but also of the caves and creeks and canyons – have been taken on trips of a day's duration at most. (Not from any lack of true pioneering instinct you understand, but rather the exigencies of lugging heavy equipment. But then again, didn't Thomas Brunner set out with three pairs of boots and sixteen pounds of tobacco???) Would we, I wonder, have had the patience and perseverance required to capture the many moods of the Paparoas on film if we had been risking our lives on rotting ladders, constructing our shelter from scratch every night, subsisting on a diet of fern root, mussels and sea-eggs, and remaining continuously wet for a week?

Which all leads me, somewhat nervously, to a third issue. When considering what Heaphy, Brunner and Haast included in their journals we need to remember that they

Chasm in shore platform.

32

Kelp in a surge pool.

Coastal woollyhead.

were all commissioned by the Nelson Provincial Government (in those days the West Coast south to the Grey River was part of Nelson) to make factual reports on unexplored parts of the province. Was the land suitable for agriculture? Could the forests be utilised for timber? Were the river bars negotiable by ships of a reasonable size? What were the prospects for finding gold or mining coal? Although in the event their accounts wandered far more extensively over both the landscape and their own feelings about it, objective reporting remained a very conscious priority.

Thus, for example, when Thomas Brunner emerged from five long desperate months struggling down the gorges of the Buller River and set out on his second journey southwards along the Paparoa coastline, he absolved himself from providing a description for public consumption on the grounds that "the character and features of the country were fully described by Mr Heaphy" on their previous visit, and that he had nothing to add "except a few personal incidents, the relation of which would interest no-one". (Maybe so; but I think I for one would very much like to have heard them!) In similar vein (but nonetheless managing to include a very full account of the "personal incident") Haast concluded his description of another harrowing episode on the Miko Cliffs (occasioned this time by a member of the party whose giddiness "endangered not merely his own life, but also the lives of those who assisted him"), with the following explanation: "I do not relate this incident for the purpose of giving interest to my narrative, or to show the dangers of travelling round this rugged coast, but merely to warn persons who have not steady heads and sure footing against attempting this route". (Come on Julius, be honest! Not want to give interest to your narrative? You of all people?)

Do we not sometimes put too much store on matters of fact in the way we relate to land? Are there not other kinds of response which might be equally, or even more, important? When I encounter passages like those above I am reminded of of the botanist who takes me to task for describing a plant growing in a seemingly impossible site as "heroic" ("Plants don't have emotions!"); or the geologist who objects to the intrusion of poetry and whimsical metaphor into my amateur attempts to describe the evolution of rocks and landforms ("Geology is a science not a poetic indulgence"); or perhaps the guide who insists on walking in front to show us the "safe route", and whose commentary is generally confined to things like "this tree is a rata, that boulder is granite, Charles Heaphy and Thomas Brunner passed this way with a Maori called Kehu and another called Tau on the 18th of May, 1846. . ."

I would like to return briefly to a book I mentioned before called ARCTIC DREAMS. It is what Richard Leakey called "an extraordinary narrative", wandering across one of the most vast and difficult terrains on earth, describing and recording many things but always preoccupied with the question of how we relate to land. Not only the obvious "we" (those of similar background and culture) but also the indigenous inhabitants and a whole range of other sentient creatures which live in, or migrate to, the arctic (polar bears, narwhals, musk-oxen, snow-geese etc.). In a chapter entitled "The Country of the Mind", Barry Lopez pauses to gather a few strands of thought which have been drifting about the tundra and pack-ice throughout all he has had to say up to this point: "What one thinks of any region, while travelling through, consists of at least three things: what one knows, what one imagines, and how one is disposed." Although knowledge is put first, and although the book is full of information of all kinds, it seems clear that its true focus lies elsewhere – on his "arctic dreams"; or, as the subtitle explains, on "imagination and desire" in this northern landscape. Not knowledge, imagination and desire; just the two that he ultimately regards as his most significant personal resourses in relating to the wild country through which he makes his journeys.

Coastal platform detail.

I turned towards these matters "somewhat nervously" a few paragraphs back not because I need any convincing that imagination and disposition are not often (usually?) far more significant than knowledge in determining the way we feel about a particular landscape, but simply because I find it very difficult to analyse or explain in words what I mean by concepts like "imagination". What lies out there in the "landscape of the mind"? I think of things like the depths of the forest at dusk, the interior of caves, the crest of the Paparoa Range waiting for the mists to rise. I think of the bottom of Truman Track, and of wondering how far down into the unseen depths the strange sculptures continue. I think of countless other hidden places throughout this limestone landscape. And I think of the kind of photographs included in this book.

Imagination is Julius Haast standing on Point Elizabeth and dreaming of distant shores. Or Charles Heaphy envisaging a "boat harbour" in a deserted Tauranga Bay. (Tauranga means "a sheltered anchorage" and Heaphy may have just been showing his knowledge of Maori nomenclature; but I think an expansion of the passage I quoted at the start of this essay shows otherwise: "Immediately below was the picturesque boat harbour of Tauranga . . . wanting but a cutter or a schooner anchored in it to give interest to and complete one of the prettiest views in the world"). It is surely the imaginative dimensions that I constantly build both onto my own experience of this coast and the personalities of my "travelling companions" which enables me to re-read their journals again and again with no lessening of interest. And it is the paths followed by my imagination which guarantee that I never get bored with a walk on Pororari Beach, a return to the coast at the bottom of Truman Track, or my umpteenth visit out to the Pancake Rocks.

I know more or less the age of the limestone in these Pancake Rocks. (Or rather geologists tell me it is 30-odd million years, and I trust their dating techniques. But can

Oystercatcher footprints.

I really say that I "know" the age of these rocks when I have great difficulty in beginning to imagine a time span of this size?) I know something of the probable sedimentary environment, the rate of uplift, the weathering and erosion of the softer and harder layers, and the kind of wave action that has possibly fashioned the stacks. I know too that the surge-pools are old collapsed caves, and that the purple algae covering the rocks near the low-water mark is known as corraline paint. I know that white-fronted terns nest here on the outer ledges. And that yellow-flowering woollyhead and shore koromiko grow in crevices between the layers of rock.

I know too, but in a somewhat more personal way, that the character and atmosphere of places like Dolomite Point can vary immensely with the lighting, the state of the tide, and the wrath of the seas. And that sometimes out there on the headland itself the age of the rocks and the rate of uplift seem to be of no consequence whatsoever. Especially on those elemental days when angry westerly gales happen to coincide with the peak of spring tides . . . with perhaps shafts of occasional sunlight breaking through banks of ominous black clouds . . . and the seas limey and full of froth after days of heavy rain . . . and great rumblings and sighings in hidden chasms beneath my feet . . . and the air wild and wet with fountains of salt spray. I know too that if at such times a voice at my shoulder should begin to say something like "the limestone here has an average calcium carbonate content of about 90% and in spite of the name doesn't actually contain any dolomite . . ." I would try to ignore it. Or say as patiently as I could that it wasn't important, not just then. Or maybe simply "Listen!" And yet I know that on other occasions I would be grateful for this kind of information. Perhaps because the better we get to know a piece of country (or a person, a painting, a photograph, a poem, an explorer's journal) the greater our scope is for imaginative journeys, if we choose to make them.

It is knowledge, I suspect, which gives us security in landscape, but imagination which makes the relationship worthwhile. What then of the way we are disposed? I have already peered some way into this labyrinth in reflecting on "distance from home" and have no real plans to explore much further for the moment, at least in this essay. All the same, it is surely self-evident that the character and mood of a particular landscape can have an enormous influence on our feelings, not only about the place in question but also about ourselves. Conversely, the disposition we arrive with inevitably governs the way we relate to land. (Remember Lopez's "reluctant traveller brooding about events at home (and) oblivious to the landscape"?) I know too that we can deliberately use landscape to alter out disposition, and in my own case, when resident at Punakaiki, any "brooding about events at home" (or abroad) can often be solved or dissolved, at least partially, by a run up the canyon of Bullock Creek or a walk along Pororari Beach. What makes the relationship complex of course is the fact that not only are we a rather temperamental species, but so is the land. And unlike a photograph, a painting, or an explorer's diary, a landscape can alter almost out of recognition with changes in the weather, the seasons or even the time of day.

All afternoon it has been raining heavily, but towards dusk the rain eases and away in the west the sky lightens considerably. Grateful for the reprieve I whistle up Rastus (to whom sandy collisions of land and sea are always the best of all possible worlds) and away we go for a walk on the beach. Heading out through the whispering toetoe and flax along the south bank of the Pororari River now running high and swift and dark muddy brown. Once out on the beach itself the choice is southwards towards Dolomite Point, past the little settlement nestling beneath towering bluffs, past drawn curtains, people at table, the blue light of the TV news; or northwards along the sandspit to where the Pororari River makes its final bend to the sea against a high buffer of sandstone cliffs. By mutual agreement man and dog set off northwards in a temporary token renunciation of civilisation. On the right, across the small tidal lagoon, are the entrances to the canyons of the Pororari River and Bullock Creek, a few hundred metres apart. Though darkness is gathering in the depths of these canyons their bold vertical bluffs and angled talus slopes are still quite distinct. To the left the surf continually pounds the steep-shelving beach, leaving huge deposits of knee-deep foam in the wake of the retreating tide. Ahead, in the fluted cliffs above the outlet of the river and running round towards the high platforms at the bottom of Truman Track, large dark patches stain the lighter sandy brown where water seeps perpetually from dense thickets of cliff-top flax. Detached from these cliffs the solitary outlier of the Maori Chief's Head contends with both the waves and the last swirlings of the escaping river. A single shag on a roost in the lagoon; three black oyster-catchers scuttling across the sandspit; a brief snatch of song from the shadowy forest.

Shapes, imaginings and journeys by the sea. I wonder what all this looked like at the end of the last ice age, when sea levels were something like 100 metres lower than they are today. Or earlier still, when the bluffs atop the present high coastal escarpment were first beginning to emerge from the waves. What lies beneath the sand at my feet, the waves beating against the cliffs, the dense forest on the hill slopes across the lagoon? What stories could that ancient rata tell? What does this patient shag make of it all?

I wonder where Charlie and Tom will try to ford the river. And if Julius has got held up again with that chap who hasn't a head for heights. To keep myself company and give them a beacon I light a small fire out of twigs of dry driftwood. Where shall I take them tomorrow? Up one of these canyons they don't seem to be all that fussed about? Or out onto Dolomite Point? (I'd particularly like to hear what Julius has got to say about those strange platey rocks right out on the end.) Perhaps we'll just give

Cliff detail.

Bull kelp on a gravel beach.

ourselves a well-earned rest, let Kehu catch some wekas and Charlie get up to date with that diary of his. Gently meandering thoughts at the end of another long day. I gaze into the flames. Listen to the waves bashing on the beach. Give Rastus a pat. Wonder if our images will draw others into this limestone landscape as the scribblings of my fellow travellers have managed to draw me. Into this landscape. And perhaps beyond. Where we can point you. But only you can go.

Fluted limestone cliffs below Truman Track, evening light.

OPPOSITE: Patterns of erosion formed by wave action in a mudstone platform near Seal Island.

Sea-cliffs below Truman Track.

Limestone blocks on the beach near Seal Island.

OPPOSITE: Spacious coastal overhang near Perpendicular Point, used as a shelter since Maori times.

Chasm leading to the main blowhole, Pancake Rocks, Punakaiki.

Main surge-pool, Dolomite Point.

Algae patterns on the dank wall of a coastal chasm.

OPPOSITE: Limestone accretions with mosses and algae in a coastal cavern below Truman Track.

Coastal flax, Dolomite Point.

Pancake Rocks, Punakaiki.

Granite and mudstone boulders beneath mudstone cliffs.

Limestone blocks on the beach near Seal Island.

Driftwood on a tidal platform.

OPPOSITE: Seaward end of the Miko Cliffs, Perpendicular Point.

Inside the tidal defile at the mouth of Bullock Creek.

Although it is very rare to find a large healthy colony of burrowing petrels on a mainland location anywhere, the coastal limestone hills immediately south of the Punakaiki River contain such a colony. Indeed, this is the only breeding place in the world of the distinctive Westland Black Petrel Procellaria westlandica, which gives them a special status among the original inhabitants of this region. They are winter breeders, and from early autumn onwards return from the sea at dusk and crash land through (or into) the forest canopy in the vicinity of their burrows. Choice of site is in part governed by the fact that these large oceanic birds are clumsy on land and need to launch themselves from cliffs or climb trees to get airborne, although once in the air the have a beautiful gliding flight.

SYNCLINE, PLATEAU AND CANYON

ALL the earliest travellers along the Paparoa coastline, both Maori and European, had little alternative but to follow a route which stayed close to the sea, where food sources were not only more diverse than further inland but usually much more reliable. Although this coastal route involved regular stretches of comparatively easy beach walking (some of which were quite long, others lamentably brief), it also included a whole string of the kind of major obstacle touched on in the previous essay. Chief among these was a series of high and precipitous headlands. But there were also very awkward sections of rocky coast where because of either unscalable cliffs or impenetrable forest there was no real choice but to struggle slowly over or around the rocks. And everything was very much at the mercy of the size of the breakers, the state of the tides, the condition of the rivers and the presence or absence of structures, devices or bits of track left by those who had gone before.

As Europeans began to travel this way more regularly the rugged nature of the coastal country gave little cause to believe that any better access might be available. But when 5000 gold miners descended on Brighton at the mouth of the Fox River late in 1866 a search was begun to find an easier route. As luck would have it, the narrowing canyon of the Fox River and even tighter defile of Dilemma Creek (the first significant southern tributary of the Fox) were found to lead to a series of inland basins of surprisingly gentle contour, extending southwards as far as the Punakaiki River. Accordingly, a horse track was soon constructed along this route, and although very much at the mercy of flooded rivers (especially in the Fox itself which was impassable during or after heavy rain, and in Dilemma Creek where the canyon was so narrow and sheer that "no track could be maintained"), the Razorback Road (now the Inland Pack Track) remained the principal route for coastal journeys between Greymouth and Westport for half a century, until bit by bit the more precipitous sections of the coastline were overcome and the Coast Road finally opened to motor vehicles in 1929.

The difficulties faced by these early travellers gives a key to understanding the nature and overall structure of the western Paparoa karst region. What appears to have happened is that earth movements associated with the uplift of the mountain ranges have buckled the land west of the Paparoa Range, raising the edges of the limestone beds and forcing the centre to warp downwards to form a broad, shallow trough or "syncline" running more or less parallel to the coast. In the bed of this

Climbing rata vine.

OPPOSITE: Bullock Creek after rain.

syncline younger sediments (sandstones, mudstones and gravels) still overlie the limestone beds in many places. But on the steep inland side and gently tilted plateaux rising towards the coast erosion has removed most of these younger rocks exposing the limestone as the present parent material over large areas.

Along the western edge the ranks of coastal bluffs are the result of uplift along a faultline coupled with the dramatic fluctuations in sea levels which have accompanied the major climatic changes of the past two million years. Viewed from the crest of the Paparoa Range, however, these coastal bluffs are concealed, and the most obvious scars of uplift and erosion are associated with the main rivers draining the western flanks of the range. Older than the earth movements which raised up the limestone beds, these rivers have been forced to cut narrow gorges on the inland side of the syncline and deep canyons through the tilted western edge to maintain their outlets to the sea.

In the tightest of these canyons (the Fox and Pororari rivers, Bullock and Dilemma creeks) sheer walls soar up to 250 m above the riverbed, sometimes directly from the water's edge but usually from a lushly-forested slope of talus debris. At first sight these walls appear to be a rather uniform greyish-white in colour, but as the eye slowly adjusts to the surroundings subtler shades of cream, pink and orange become apparent, with whole faces sometimes transformed into vivid whites and golds when catching the morning or evening sun. On the floors of the canyons the rivers and streams meander and tumble in a pattern of rapids, clear shoals of sparkling granite boulders, and deep mysterious pools. In places the beds may be wholly or partially blocked by huge slabs dislodged from the rim of the canyon walls, perhaps in some bygone earth tremor, or perhaps just cast adrift from the parent mass when the slow process of rainwater dissolution reached the critical limit. At times too some of these rivers escape to underground channels, as Bullock Creek does most of the time, Dilemma Creek does with reasonable regularity, and even the main branch of the Fox River can in times of minimal rainfall.

Today good foot tracks (Fox, Pororari), an old bush tramway (Tiropahi) and farm roads (Bullock Creek, Punakaiki, Nile) provide easy access into or through all of these major river systems. For those already familiar with the roads and tracks a scramble along the beds of the rivers and streams themselves usually provides more constant contact with sculpted rock and more open vistas of encircling cliffs than the periodic glimpses available from the tracks along the forested banks. (Lest this be misinterpreted, it should be added that the forests covering the banks and talus slopes are one of the main attractions of any canyon walk; but tracks buried in forest inevitably by-pass other landscape features.) Similar rewards can often be found by turning aside into clefts and gaps in the canyon walls, although in places thick tangles

Spider orchid Corybas sp. on moss-covered limestone slabs, Waggon Creek.

Bearded orchid Calochilus paludosus on pakihi, Four Mile.

Perching orchid Earina mucronata, Pororari River Track.

of kiekie and supplejack, dense patches of nettles and lurking slots in the ground can provide some minor discouragement. And for the really adventurous there is endless scope for exploration further away from the tracks and streambeds in the confusing jumble of dissected ridges, abandoned valleys and old clogged sinkholes which make up the uneven surface of the karstfields between the main river canyons. In this bewildering and densely-forested terrain, where horizons are non-existent and navigation always difficult, it takes no great effort to get yourself lost. Thus, although some purists might quibble with the choice of words, it does seem to us to have many of the intrinsic qualities of true wilderness, albeit lying within only a few kilometres of a main highway.

Some of the more striking features of the main canyons are repeated on a much more intimate scale in the smaller creeks and tributary streams which wend across this karst landscape. One very obvious difference, however, is that many of these side-creeks are confined to the limestone region, and as a result carry only minimal quantities of boulders and gravel. This in turn means a general reduction in the processes of mechanical erosion, and corresponding increase in the influence of the dissolving powers of water in shaping the beds and banks. And it also ensures that most of the contemporary sculpture along these smaller streams is more or less continually out on display, not hidden away under unknown depths of imported gravels, as happens in all the main rivers along those sections where they cut through the uplifted limestone beds.

Many of these smaller creeks sooner or later become impassable on account of waterfalls, deep chasms, or places where the stream vanishes into, or emerges from, underground channels. But before this happens the beds and banks usually manage to display all manner of marvellous rills, runnels, rifts, tilted slabs, tumbled blocks, natural weirs, erratic channels and symmetrical cauldrons and bowls, with themes often reminiscent of the Pancake Rocks, as the etching waters continually highlight a very regular and even pattern in the sedimentary layers. Inevitably much of the rock along the beds and banks of these streams is coated in colourful algae or dense carpets of mosses, liverworts and other pioneering plants. Higher on the banks flowering herbs like native foxgloves grow abundantly in moist and shady places, ferns and treeferns flourish on every hand, and the larger trees regularly meet overhead to canopy the creek bed. In many places this combination of moss and sculpted rock, fern and forest giant produces an enchantment beyond the reach of words, while the winding course most of these streams seem to follow ensures that some new surprise awaits discovery each time you round another corner in the creek bed.

On the gentler contours across the bed of the syncline streams appear to behave more normally. But appearances can be deceptive in limestone country, and these phases of apparently normal flow often last only as far as the next eccentric flourish. Bullock Creek is perhaps the classic example. As it crosses the cleared farmland it flows over a gently meandering bed of sand and gravels. But where it meets the limestone outcrops on the western side of the farm the waters plunge into underground channels and flow southwards to join the Pororari River by way of Cave Creek, leaving the bed of Bullock Creek completely dry, at all events until it begins to gather water from other sources further down the gorge. In times of heavy rain however these underground channels quickly fill to capacity, and Bullock Creek floods swiftly and frighteningly through this otherwise dry section of its bed, inundating its upper gorge and swamp and pouring into the entrances of several other cave networks downstream from the usual points of submergence.

In this striking example of "up-valley retreat", which is typical of drainage patterns in many karst regions, the upper gorge of Bullock Creek and its normally dry caves are all parts of an older system of plumbing which has now been abandoned except in times of flood. It is a process which is being repeated (although usually less obviously) all over the face of this complex karst region, and indeed has been going on for hundreds of thousands of years. As long as the land continues to rise (and scientists calculate the present rate of uplift at Punakaiki to be something like 27 mm per thousand years), and as long as some remnants of limestone survive in these parts, the waters flowing off or through this karst landscape will continue to dissolve more rock and create new landforms, as diverse in detail and yet as similar in basic theme as the great river canyons which dissect the whole region, and the miniature rills and runnels which etch away the surfaces of individual rock outcrops.

Streambed, Welsh Creek.

Outcrops of papa mudstone, Awakiri River.

Fox River Canyon.

Bullock Creek after rain.

Streambed inside the Hole in the Wall.
OPPOSITE: Hole in the Wall, Nile River.

Small rapids and pool near the resurgence of Waggon Creek.

Limestone bridges, Waggon Creek.

Natural weir in small limestone creek.

Currents and eddies of river foam.

OPPOSITE and ABOVE: Karren surfaces on large streambed limestone blocks, Bullock Creek.

Images of eroded streamside limestone from the Fox River narrows near Dilemma Creek.

Supplejack tangles, Fox River Track.

Beech forest, Fox River.

Waterfall in a tributary stream of Dilemma Creek.

Beech forest on the bed of the syncline.

Forested banks, Waggon Creek.

Wind-blasted rimu on coastal hills.

Relic of the gold rush era – the Argyle Dam, Four Mile Road.

CAVES IN THE PAPAROA SYNCLINE

M ANY caves are already known to exist in the limestone country between Charleston and Punakaiki, and it is anybody's guess what others will come to light once the forbidding surface of the karst plateau between the major rivers becomes more systematically explored. At present all known caves in the region are on the western side of the syncline where the relatively gentle dip of the limestone beds has ensured that the development of the underground patterns of drainage has been mainly along horizontal weaknesses in the rock. In most of the major caves, however, passages and galleries have formed at several different levels, and as a result quite complex systems have evolved, with the horizontal sections linked to each other by a variety of vertical shafts, winding stairways, mudslides and underground mountains of slab debris accumulated from the collapse of former ceilings.

Sometimes the presence of these caves is indicated on the surface by imposing entrance arches, but in other instances the way in from the outside world may be no more than a shaft or ominously gloomy pit on the forest floor, or a log-jam in a streambed or at the bottom of some overgrown sinkhole. Inside these often uninviting entrances, cave interiors frequently come to a swift and muddy halt, while others may continue for several kilometres (the longest is about 8 km) through an underground landscape which ranges from twisting keyhole passages and tight muddy squeezes to large cavernous halls and lovely decorated galleries. Most of these western Paparoa caves are still linked to active rivers and streams and are thus subject to frequent overload flooding. Besides being very hazardous for cavers, these floods also regularly produce significant alterations to the subterranean topography, as swollen streams laden with silt and forest debris sluice through the passages, clearing away blockages from one part of the system only to seal up slots and openings somewhere else.

Over long periods of time the streams which form caves gradually seek out deeper and more direct routes through a limestone region. As this process advances, older passages and caverns at higher levels are increasingly left clear of flooding, and eventually become "dry caves". In a damp climate however, minor drips and trickles will usually continue to seep down through the cracks and joints in the roof and walls into these drier parts of the cave, and where this occurs, cave formations are likely to develop.

When a drop of percolating water pauses above an air-filled interior, minute quantities of carbon dioxide are released to the atmosphere, and the water, no longer

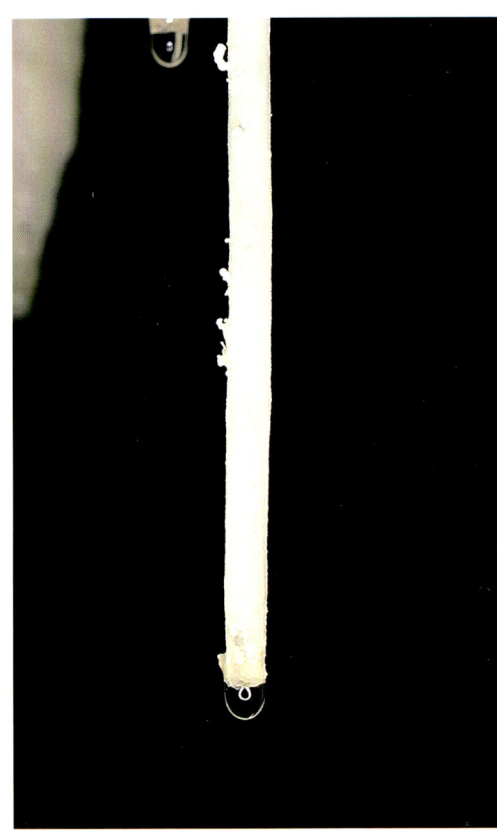

The patient work of water.

82

Cave roof, Te Tahi.

able to carry all of its dissolved calcium content, leaves a tiny deposit where it falls from the roof and again where it splashes onto the floor. Slowly, over vast periods of time, these calcite deposits build up into formations known as speleothems: brittle stalactites and stalagmites, fragile straws, weirdly shaped helictites, flowstone floors and mysterious rimstone pools. Time and gravity are the main controlling forces in the evolution of the often exquisite forms which result from this process, but delicate air currents within the cave are also responsible for some of the more eccentric flourishes, while mineral deposits leached from the soils above bring colourings of brown, pink, red, blue and black to enhance the glistening creamy-white of the pure calcite accretions. Although the results are often indescribably beautiful and bizarre, perhaps the strangest thing of all about cave formations is the fact that the same chemical process which gnaws the heart out of limestone regions is also responsible for the construction of these most exquisite and delicate of all rock sculptures. But Nature is full of subtle ironies like this – witness the fact that like some of the loveliest of wild flowers, these rarest of inanimate shapes and textures should so often occur in the least accessible places.

Adventure and aesthetics aside, limestone caves like those in the western Paparoas are also of considerable importance to science. Geologists can date speleothems by radio-isotopic means, and thus establish a range of minimum ages at which different levels in caves have dried out. In the Ananui Caves in the Charleston region this subterranean geomorphology is almost certainly related to the evolution of nearby flights of interglacial terraces. If a clear link can be established, the dates of formations within the caves could provide important new information on elusive questions like the rate of uplift of this part of the South Island, and perhaps also supply an improved time-scale for dating the warmer and cooler cycles of the last of the ice ages.

Many caves in the region also contain important deposits of subfossil bones, including extinct creatures (like several species of moa and a giant flightless goose), birds which although not extinct are now no longer found in this part of the country (including takahe, kakapo, kokako and saddleback) and remains of marine animals (like whale skeletons and sharks' teeth) caught as the land emerged from the sea. As far as living creatures are concerned, caves are often the home of an odd collection of inhabitants which have managed to adapt in curious ways to life in a constantly dark and damp environment. Contrary to popular fears and folk-tales, these cave-dwellers are almost invariably small, shy and of entirely inoffensive disposition.

There appears to be a major upsurge of interest in caving throughout New Zealand at present, and accordingly the Punakaiki region is bound to see more in the way of hard hats, muddy overalls and carbide lamps than it has hitherto. However, it

Insect traps secreted by glow-worms.

should be added that most of the caves are unlikely to be opened up to casual visitors in the future, either because they are too difficult and dangerous, or simply because they are too fragile and vulnerable. The 130 m or so of safe, modestly-decorated passage of the upper Fox River Cave, which has been visited by tourists since late last century, is still the best place in the region to satisfy initial curiosity about the type of landforms found beneath the ground. Beyond this, no great decorated vault has so far come to light in the Paparoas suitable for conversion into a major tourist cave, although there is some feeling that parts of the 8 km Ananui Caves (the Maori name means "big cave"; cavers renamed them "The Metro") near Charleston might serve this purpose. But if this were to happen it would need to be done with very careful planning and control, since these caves already bear considerable scars from having been "opened up" in the 1960s. Perhaps the strongest argument against such a course however is that the opening up of a tourist cave near Charleston or Punakaiki would inevitably divert some of the interest from Karamea's excellent Honeycomb Hill Caves. And in these difficult economic times Karamea needs such a special attraction to tempt travellers to make the 200 km detour from the main tourist route along the Paparoa coastline and up the Buller Gorge.

Nor will it necessarily follow from the creation of a new national park in the region that its caves will be made more accessible to those accustomed to finding their own way through difficult country. There are hazards aplenty in most caves at the best of times, and few people are aware of the frightening speed at which many of the passages in the western Paparoas can flood, or how much difference there can be between the amount of rain falling at the coast and in the catchments of some of the streams which drain through the caves. Early in 1987 eight people were rescued from a flooded Babylon Cave in the Fox River, a cave previously thought to have been more or less safe from the threat of flooding. Had the party (which was well-equipped and contained several experienced cavers) chosen that same day to visit a cave like Xanadu in Bullock Creek instead of Babylon, the outcome might easily have been tragic.

The best advice to those keen on exploring the hidden world beneath the surface of this limestone landscape is always to consult a ranger or experienced caver before attempting to visit any cave. Or, better still, join a caving club. These clubs not only possess a very necessary store of experience and local knowledge, but are also ready to provide instruction, advise on equipment and organise expeditions. Clubs based in Westport, Christchurch and Nelson are all presently very active in the Punakaiki-Charleston region, exploring more extensively the known cave systems and prospecting for new ones, in what is proving to be probably the most exciting period ever for caving on the West Coast.

Organ pipes, Xanadu.

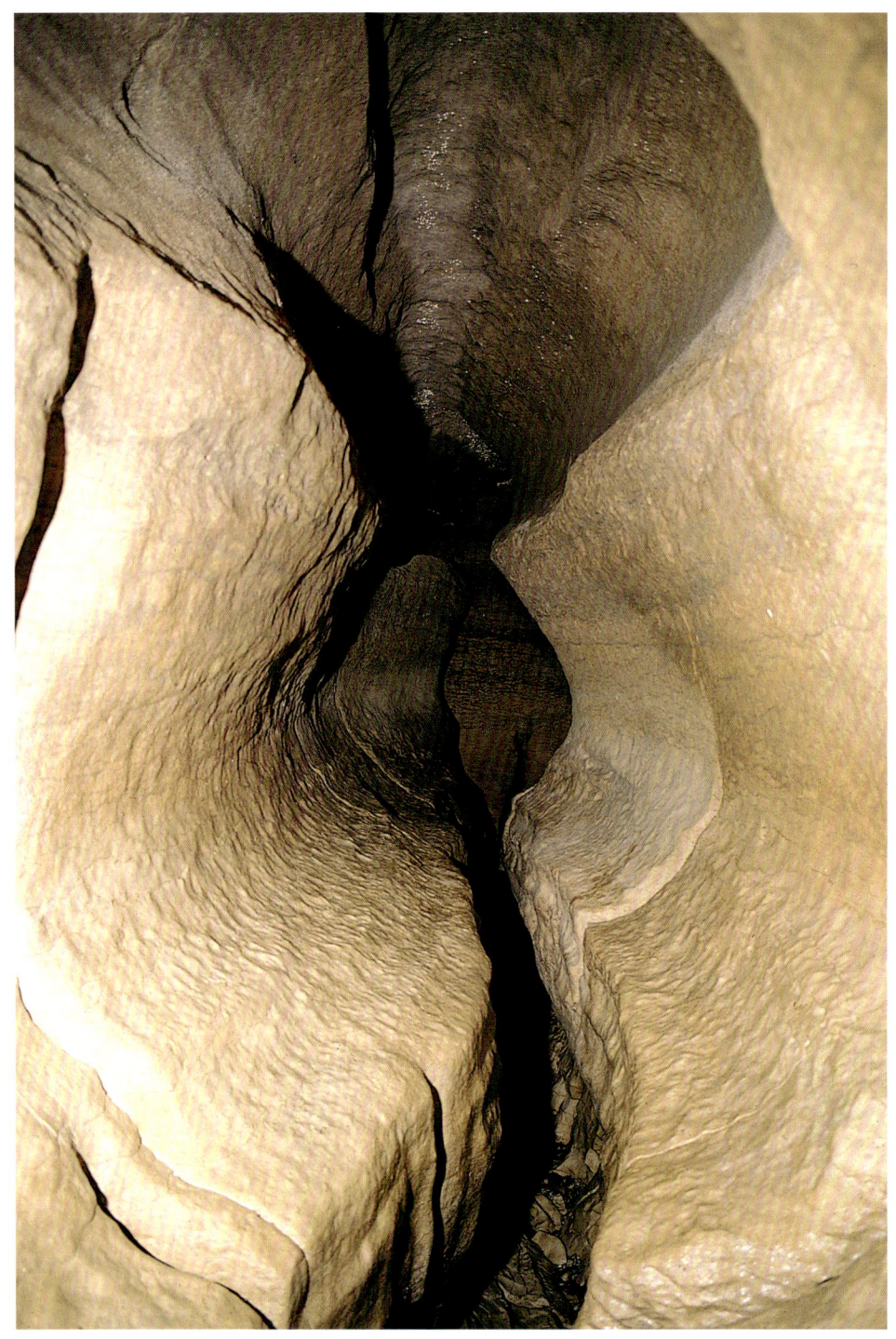

Typical keyhole passage, Xanadu.

Flowstone floor in a small unnamed cave, Waggon Creek.

Cave pearls, Xanadu roof.

Wall of a shallow streamside cave, Waggon Creek.

Cave formations, Te Tahi.

Cave formations, Te Tahi.

Mineral colouring leached from the forest floor.

Decorated gallery, Te Tahi.

BEYOND THE LIMESTONE LANDSCAPE

ALTHOUGH our main purpose in this book has been to try to convey something of the deeper character of the western Paparoa karst region, it has never been our intention to limit our focus to the limestone landscape alone. Right from the beginning we have found it impossible to dissociate our journeys through the western lowlands from our ascents onto the crest of the Paparoa Range itself. Indeed, some of the most rewarding of all our photographic explorations have been among the granitic crags and misty tarns of this coastal chain of mountains, and near and beyond the treeline we have consistently encountered shapes and settings and atmosphere which have been just as enticing as subjects for artistic photography as the limestone eccentricities of the coast and caves and canyons.

The other main reason for giving some exposure to the Paparoa mountains is simply that despite their very obvious appeal for wilderness tramping (described by Les Molloy in OUTDOOR RECREATION ON THE WEST COAST as offering a challenge to the alpine traveller "unsurpassed in any other range of equivalent height outside Fiordland"), they remain so little known. To some extent this would seem to be the result of a general absence of tracks leading onto the tops, and of huts near or above the bushline, both of which are found only at the northern (Buckland Peaks) and southern (Croesus) limits of the range. But even as a more distant profile, the jagged crest of the main coastal chain often escapes notice, partly because of a local cloud cover which rises out of the western lowlands and regularly blankets the summits through the middle part of the day, but partly too because the often abrupt country bordering the coastal highway grants only limited glimpses of the craggy Paparoa skyline.

As in the case of the surrounding lowlands, the character of the Paparoa alpine scenery is very much the product of its underlying geology. Most of the central parts of the range have been fashioned out of a hard, banded granitic gneiss, a very ancient (700 million years) metamorphic rock which is amongst the oldest of all rocks found in New Zealand. Along with other Paparoa basement rocks (coarse younger granites further to the north, very old greywackes in the south) this ancient gneiss shares no kinship whatsoever with the rocks of the Southern Alps, but is closely related to those of more distant Fiordland and Stewart Island, from which the whole northwestern corner of the South Island has gradually slipped apart along the Alpine Fault over the past 25 million years.

Silver beech and mountain neinei at the treeline.

Characteristic red tufted foliage of mountain neinei.

This 480 km displacement of the Paparoa rocks from their ancestral seat is one of the more striking manifestations of New Zealand's precarious location astride a major boundary between two of the Earth's great crustal plates. But in spite of this distant exile the old kinship between the Fiordland and Paparoa ranges remains apparent in the contemporary landforms. To quote Les Molloy again: "On closer inspection the central spine of the (Paparoa) range is seen to be an amazing chain of flat-topped peaks, sharp crags, gendarmes, cirques and bluffs carved by glacial action from the hard granite and gneiss. . . The similarities between the crest of the range and Fiordland are striking."

Similar parallels are found immediately east of the main range where the deep longitudinal valleys of the Ohikanui and Otututu with their hanging side-valleys and truncated spurs bear testimony to occupation by major rivers of ice at some time in the past, with much the same results as in the glaciated Fiordland valleys. To the casual eye the most striking difference between these valleys and those of the Southern Alps (which have also been heavily glaciated) is the general absence in the Paparoa and Fiordland mountains of the huge volumes of frost-shattered rock which dominate so much of the South Island high country scenery as screes and gravels.

Photographs convey far better than words can the general character of this Paparoa alpine region – the bold outline of the ridgecrest crags, the impenetrable tangles of leatherwood scrub, the serene setting of the graceful little tarns, the swards of lawn-like carpet grass, the softening charms of the delicate alpine flowers, the wonderful interplays of light cast by the rising and setting sun, and perhaps most of all, the veils of mist and fingers of swirling cloud which from time to time creep up from the valleys and envelop the summit ridges. Sometimes this invasion of mist arrives on the tops with little warning making alpine travel difficult if not downright dangerous, and more than once in our traverses along the range we have set out in the serene light of a clear dawn only to arrive later in the morning at a point on a misty Paparoas ridge where rocks tossed into the clammy gloom in three directions have indicated with the authority of a celestial command that remaining exactly where we are, or cautiously retracing our steps, are the only courses left open to us.

And yet, like the wild storms which batter the coast, the mists and clouds which hang about these summit ridges bring with them moments of special magic. In misty conditions features like crags and tarns are transformed from familiar landforms into surreal images. Lichens, mosses and tussocks seem to freshen and find new life in the moist atmosphere and filtered light. And if the cloud cover extends down to the bushline, gnarled beeches and skeletal dracophyllums take on the spectral shapes of forests of myth and fairy tale. Silence too seems somehow more intense, and isolated sounds like the cry of a goat or kea, or the tinkle of falling water, emerge strangely amplified from the shrouds of grey nothingness which border the immediate circle of visible things.

In contrast, mornings and evenings often leave the tops clear, and one of the great delights of tramping this range is to camp within a short scramble of a prominent Paparoas peak in order to witness the light plays of dawn and dusk. First light regularly provides lovely panoramas of blue ranges receding away to the east, forming a great sweep from the Tasman Mountains in the north to the ice summits of Mounts Cook and Tasman away to the south. In the evening this land to the east is slowly swallowed by shadows while on the western side of the range the sun often dips beneath the banks of clouds, illuminating the sea and highlighting the entrances to the main river canyons. With the intervening lowlands also slipping into shadows beneath thin veils of smoky evening mist, these canyons appear like notches in the rim of some great ancient shield, left abandoned after long battles against the armies of erosion, but still somehow managing to protect the fragile country behind from other kinds of incursion.

As the peaks of the Paparoa Range itself shed the last of the sunlight, the higher, ice-bound summits away to the south hold it a moment longer. Perhaps it is fitting that they should do so, for most of us cannot escape a sense of awe at the sight of these loftiest of New Zealand mountains, even as a distant prospect. But inspiring as they are, they give us little present cause for envy. From where we stand on our less elevated Paparoa eyrie exhilaration and adventure still seem to beckon from the high granite ridges on every hand, while endless wonder and enchantment inhabit the limestone country veiled in its forests and shadows beneath our feet.

Such moments have a powerful spiritual significance, and I have always found it difficult to watch a dawn or sunset from the crest of the Paparoa Range without finding my thoughts stealing off to overviews of a different sort: to the way we think of wilderness; to the value we place on those parts of our land which are still wild and unspoilt; and to the kinds of places this whole planet so urgently needs to preserve, not only for our own escape, adventure and enrichment, but also for plants and animals whose tenure long predates our own, but who cannot speak for themselves. Or, to borrow those oft-quoted lines of Gerard Manley Hopkins, which, although written on the other side of the world, are nonetheless so utterly appropriate in their sentiments and sprung rhythm to the kind of country we have been travelling in all the pages of this book:

"What would the world be, once bereft
Of wet and of wildness? Let them be left,
O let them be left, wildness and wet;
Long live the weeds and the wilderness yet."

Alpine cushion Donatia novae-zelandiae in flower.

Evening cloud rolls in from the sea to blanket the Paparoa lowlands.

Looking east from Mt Faraday at sunrise.

First light on the crest of the Paparoa Range.

The large-flowered mat daisy Raoulia grandiflora on granite barrens, Buckland Peaks.

OPPOSITE: Large mountain daisy and musk daisy mat, Mt Lavoisier.

Alpine gentian and mat daisy, Mt Faraday.

OPPOSITE: Contorted trunk of southern rata, Buckland Peaks track.

OPPOSITE and ABOVE: Silver beech forest interiors near the treeline.

OPPOSITE and ABOVE: Alpine tarn, Mt Faraday.

OPPOSITE and ABOVE: Alpine tarn, Mt Faraday.

Large boulder with mosses and alpine herbs.

Afternoon cloud on the crest of the Paparoa Range.

Jumble of granite ridges at the head of the Ohikanui Valley.

Buckland Peaks granite.

113

A natural ruin of granite slabs, Buckland Peaks.

The Buckland Peaks in a typical veil of mist.

Dracophyllum and tussock on a windswept ridgecrest.
OPPOSITE: Lichen-encrusted granite, Three Sisters.

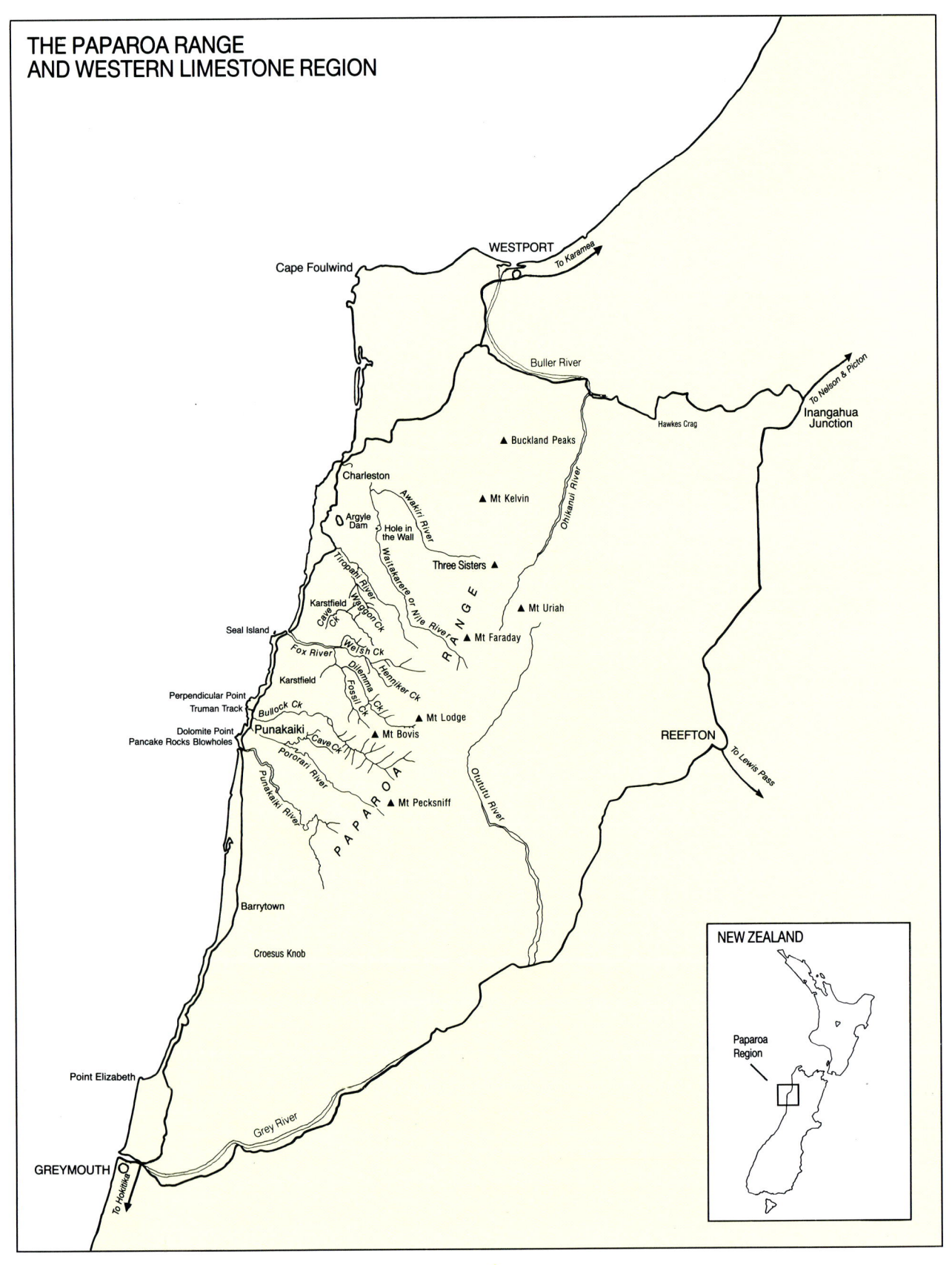

THE PAPAROA RANGE
AND WESTERN LIMESTONE REGION

WESTPORT
Cape Foulwind
To Karamea
Buller River
Hawkes Crag
To Nelson & Picton
Inangahua Junction
▲ Buckland Peaks
Charleston
Argyle Dam
Awakiri River
Hole in the Wall
▲ Mt Kelvin
Ohikanui River
Three Sisters ▲
Tiropahi River
Waggon Ck
Karstfield
Cave Ck
Seal Island
Welsh Ck
Fox River
Waitakere or Nile River
R A N G E
▲ Mt Uriah
▲ Mt Faraday
Henniker Ck
Karstfield
Dilemma Ck
Fossil Ck
Perpendicular Point
Truman Track
Bullock Ck
▲ Mt Lodge
Dolomite Point
Punakaiki
Cave Ck
▲ Mt Bovis
Pancake Rocks Blowholes
REEFTON
To Lewis Pass
Pororari River
Ohikaiti River
P A P A R O A
Punakaiki River
▲ Mt Pecksniff
Barrytown
Croesus Knob
Point Elizabeth
Grey River
GREYMOUTH
To Hokitika

NEW ZEALAND
Paparoa Region